C000085700

TUBE STATION
TRIVIA

CAPITAL HISTORY

Contents

ISBN 978-1-85414-431-7

First published 2018

Published by Capital History
www.capitalhistory.london

Printed in the EU

Thanks are extended to Trevor Baker, Dave Green, David Leboff and Kim Rennie for
assistance with suggesting items of trivia for this book.

Photo credits
All photos are by the author except:
Capital Transport: 19, 28, 29, 31, 32, 47, 49, 61, 63, 65, 69, 71, 72, 73, 80

INTRODUCTION

In 2003 I first attempted what has come to be known as the "Tube Challenge" - a record included in World Record books that involves travelling through every Underground station on the network in the fastest time possible. People have been attempting this since the 1960s and it is more popular than you might think. In 2004 (on my 7th attempt) I set a record time for the 275 stations then on the Underground of 18 hours, 35 minutes and 43 seconds. The second occasion I held the record was in 2013 when there were 270 stations, which I did in a time of 16 hours, 20 minutes, 27 seconds.

It was after the second record that I realised that whilst I'd been through all the Tube stations, I hadn't got out at all of them - and so that was something that I set out to do, picking up pieces of trivia and spotting things that I'd never seen before along the way. This turned into a series of YouTube videos (with over 7 million views), which then led to this book.

Geoff Marshall
London
July 2018

BAKERLOO LINE

The Bakerloo Line was created in 1906 with its full name being the Baker Street & Waterloo Railway – a London paper took those two words as portmanteau 'Baker' and 'loo' to create a name of the line and it was soon adopted by the railway company. At one time the line used to go further north, to Watford Junction.

Elephant & Castle

At Elephant & Castle, the tunnels continue south for a few hundred yards as some work was done in the late 1940s on a planned extension to Camberwell; work stopped owing to post-war spending restraints. Unusually there are two emergency staircases at this station, one for the Bakerloo and one for the Northern. In several cases across the network the sign telling you how many steps there are is incorrect, and Elephant & Castle is an example. On the Bakerloo staircase, the sign incorrectly says that there are 124 steps, when there are in fact 117.

Lambeth North

Lambeth North holds a record for the number of renamings within a short period of time of opening. It opened as Kennington Road in March 1906, became Westminster Bridge Road just five months later, then Lambeth (North) in 1917. About ten years later it lost the brackets around North.

Waterloo

When the line was first mooted this would have been the southern terminus, hence the original name of the railway.

Charing Cross

The platform walls here are splendidly decorated with copies of parts of works of art on show in the nearby National

Gallery. The long walk from the platform to Charing Cross main line station is explained by the fact that the station was sited (and named) for Trafalgar Square when built and received a subway connection to Charing Cross in 1979. Allow five minutes for this connection if you have a train to catch.

Piccadilly Circus

When you come down the escalators towards the Piccadilly Line you'll most likely hear a busker who is performing at the bottom with the music 'floating' up at you. This location makes it one of the most sought-after spots to busk on the Underground as it earns the most money. At the bottom of the escalators, don't go straight on – turn left, and in the corridor immediately on your left you'll find a small sign saying, 'Bakerloo Line'. This takes you up a small section of the spiral staircase (the rest of which is blocked off with no access) and is a shortcut through to the Bakerloo Line. It can also obviously be used in reverse and is an excellent shortcut from the northbound Bakerloo Line platforms to the Piccadilly Line, much quicker than following the official signs.

Oxford Circus

The 1906 Leslie Green terracotta station building on one side of Argyle Street contrasts in style with the station building opposite, opened by the Central London Railway (today's Central Line) six years earlier. This is the only place where these two styles sit side by side.

Regent's Park

Like Warwick Avenue, another Bakerloo Line station with no surface building, there's a corridor that leads down from some steps to the ticket hall area. But can you also spot the entrance to the underground passageway that allows local residents-only access to the nearby gardens and leads under the Marylebone Road and into Regent's Park itself?

Baker Street

Referencing Sherlock Holmes, there are tiles on the platform here that depict the famous detective smoking his trademark pipe, but as no smoking is allowed on the Underground, it is possible (if you are lucky with lining up the shot) to take a picture from inside a train that shows the 'No Smoking' roundel sticker on a window of a train in the foreground, with Sherlock smoking a pipe in the background!

Marylebone

At Marylebone, there is a giveaway at the end of the platforms to what the Underground station was originally called, with the words 'GREAT CENTRAL' in the tiling. In 1917 it was sensibly renamed 'Marylebone' to match the main line terminus that it serves and is part of. It was the Great Central Railway that built Marylebone main line station.

Edgware Road

Edgware Road was restored in the 1990s with new tiling and booking office furniture in original style. It also has grass growing on its south wall (facing the A40) and an old 'You May Telephone from Here' sign outside – and if you have a mobile phone you can!

Paddington

The tiles along platform level here and in the area at the bottom of the escalators depict men working in a tunnelling shield, digging the Tube tunnels that the trains run along.

Warwick Avenue

This is unusual for a Bakerloo Line station in that it doesn't have a surface level building, just two subway entrances, one of which has always cut into the road.

Maida Vale

Maida Vale was entirely staffed by women when it opened during the First World War in 1915. Before that war (and after it until the Second World War), operating, station and management staff on the Underground was 100% male. The station has a beautiful mosaic Underground roundel above the staircase. If you've seen the film *Paddington* here is where the exteriors were shot for what was called *Westbourne Grove* (a mix of Westbourne Park and Ladbroke Grove stations).

> 45% of the Underground system is in tunnel.

Kilburn Park

It is worth getting off the train here and heading up towards the ticket hall with its delightful green and white tile pattern; admire the attractive roof lantern as you ride the escalators. The exterior is well worth seeing also, as one of the last terra-cotta-tiled frontages to be built for the Tube.

Queen's Park and Kensal Green

Uniquely, passengers on Bakerloo Line trains travel through a train depot on the trip between Queen's Park and Kensal Green.

Willesden Junction

An unusual station in that it has 'high level' and 'low level' platforms – both used primarily by London Overground services, but on the lower level the tracks are also shared with Bakerloo Line services. On the lower level, look out for the lesser-used Platform 2 in the middle, which is used by only two Overground trains per day, both early in the morning. A nice touch is the subway linking the high and low level platforms which is still tiled in British Rail Network SouthEast red, white and blue.

Half a million mice are estimated to live on the London Underground (rent-free).

Harlesden to Kenton

It must be said that this section of the Underground is possibly the least interesting on the system, in part due to many years of neglect from British Rail and then Silverlink Metro. All of these stations are owned by Network Rail but managed by the Underground. At Harlesden the smell of chocolate is often in the air due to the nearby biscuits factory; Stonebridge Park was the northern terminus of the line from 1982 when it was cut back from Watford Junction; the service as far as Harrow & Wealdstone was restored in 1984. At Wembley Central there is a set of stairs only ever used when there are events at Wembley Stadium.

Harrow & Wealdstone

At Harrow & Wealdstone, follow the 'step-free' way in and out of the station, and you'll see an old abandoned platform with grass now growing through it where trains used to run on a small LMS branch line to Stanmore. The section from Belmont to Stanmore closed in 1952 and the remaining part was closed as one of the Beeching cuts in 1964. For many years, Bakerloo Line trains continued from here right up to Watford Junction but since 1982 this has been as far as they go.

CENTRAL LINE

The Central Line started life in 1900 when it was opened as the Central London Railway, first operating between Shepherd's Bush and Bank. It was coloured blue on early Underground maps, and eventually grew and expanded over time to reach West Ruislip in the west and Ongar in the east. It was later cut back to Epping, which is a good place to start.

Epping

At the end of the line you'll see very clearly how people get to and from this station – by car. It has the largest car park of any station on the network with 599 spaces. But the thing to see here is the railway beyond Epping, as Underground trains used to go further up the line to Ongar. This part of the Central Line was closed in 1994. Exit the station, turn right, and you'll find a footbridge that crosses the railway. From here you can get a good view of the tracks still heading north-east. Part of the route is now operated by the Epping–Ongar Railway so you can still ride on it on certain days. Epping is the only station on the Underground that is both beyond the boundary of the M25 and within the boundary of a six-zone travelcard.

Theydon Bois

The old stationmaster's cottage still survives adjacent to the modern-day entrance. The building is easily identifiable; being painted white and lettered "Number 1, Station House".

Only a little over 10 per cent of Underground stations are south of the Thames.

Debden

In a large building adjacent to the London-bound track here is the printing works where Bank of England banknotes are printed.

Loughton

An excellent photo to get here is a line-up of platform name roundels. See if you can get an angle that lets you capture 'all four' across the platforms as it makes for a very arty picture. Then walk right to end of either one of the platforms, turn around and admire the architectural feature of the curving canopies that stretch along the platforms. These were completed by the LNER in 1940 in preparation for the take-over of the line to Ongar by the Underground. It has been suggested that the huge semi-circular window above the main entrance was influenced by the façade of the King's Cross main line terminus.

Buckhurst Hill

This part of the Central Line uses parts of what used to be the steam-operated Eastern Counties Railway, which means there are several remnants of the *old* railway to see at this end of the network. Here at Buckhurst Hill, the station house that survives to the south of the present platforms dates back to 1856. The rest of the present station though is from 1892.

Woodford

As you head south from Buckhurst Hill on your way to Woodford, look out the left-hand side, and just before you arrive at Woodford, you'll see the branch that goes off around the 'Hainault Loop' and get a glimpse of Roding Valley station.

South Woodford

The railway line here dates to Eastern Counties Railway days, and there are some small clues at this and the next station that this is the case. The most obvious (and the best) thing to see is the 1856 station building on the eastbound side at South Woodford which dates from before it became part of the Underground. Note too, the wording on the roundel here that still says, "George Lane" – one of only four Underground stations today to have a bracketed suffix on its signs.

Snaresbrook

In common with a number of other stations on the eastern end of the Central Line, the platforms here have some very attractive original features, e.g. the canopies with attractive metal brackets and, on the westbound side, the arched windows in the brickwork. Note how the concrete panels that carry some of the eastbound platform roundels have a roundel silhouette on the rear. These were provided to face a long-gone bay platform.

Roding Valley

Of all the stations on the Underground, this one is a personal favourite since it is the least used station on the Underground – it averages around 370,000 passengers a year, the great majority of which are at peak times. Come here in the middle of the day, and it's extremely likely that you'll be the only passenger getting on or off the train. Walk the length of the platforms; enjoy the quietness! And then wait for the next train to take you out of here – they run every 20 minutes out here, so you may have to be patient.

Chigwell

Here on the Hainault Loop, most inner rail trains terminate at Woodford, before reversing and heading back to Hainault, but there are a limited number of trains in the morning that carry on through to central London, which are popular with commuters. In the timetables on the walls of the ticket office here, the trains that do this are listed in red.

Grange Hill

The box-shaped ticket hall replaced the original station building here in 1948. It is somewhat similar, though on a smaller scale, to that at White City, built the previous year. The two styles of station furniture on different ends of the platforms show where they were extended when work was carried out for the introduction of Central Line trains in the 1940s.

Hainault

Hainault has an unusual claim to fame on the network, in that when the station was made step-free with lifts installed, one was put in at the ticket hall to connect with the lower landing which has a vertical rise of only 18 inches, making it the shortest distance a lift will travel overall on the Underground. It takes just three seconds to make the journey. If you use it, look carefully and you will find it is actually a 'lifting platform' and the sides of the 'car' remain static during the ascent or descent (there is a similar lift at Stratford). The large train depot to the north of the station was used by the US Army during the Second World War.

The Underground was owned by private companies until 1933, when the London Passenger Transport Board (London Transport) was formed as a nationalised concern.

Fairlop

This station is just 65 seconds from Hainault and on a clear day you can look down the perfectly straight track between the stations to watch your train arrive. An RAF airfield was built on Fairlop Plain in 1940 and it was once planned as the site of a new London airport before Heathrow was selected. One can imagine how busy this stretch of line would be had that happened.

Barkingside

Getting back onto the train, head one stop south to Barkingside, and walk over the green iron footbridge, making a note of the intricate designs contained in it as you go. Go back onto the southbound platform, and investigate the old waiting room that is still here – an original Great Eastern Railway building from over 100 years ago. Note the etched glass window signage in original style.

Newbury Park

Back on the train and heading west, the next place to alight is Newbury Park. From the platform level it seems like nothing special, but there are two things to note here. Exit the station to the street and you'll find yourself in a bus station, under a giant cavernous concrete canopy. It has a copper covered barrel-vaulted roof that won a Festival of Britain architectural award and is now Grade II listed. The bus station opened in 1949 when the Central Line first came here, but Newbury Park as a station had already existed for almost fifty years on a GER/LNER branch that connected Newbury Park with Ilford. Stand on the pavement on the busy A12 with the station across the street from you, peer over the wall and look south and you'll see the Central Line curving off to the right. But look straight on and you'll see the area where the steam trains used to run to/from Ilford and beyond. This (like many abandoned railways) has now been turned into allotments.

Gants Hill

At street level there is not much to see here, but subsurface Gants Hill is based upon similar and more elaborate designs for the Moscow subway network. Admire the spacious area in between the two platforms with the gorgeous uplighters, and look out for the small red and blue Underground roundels in the tilework.

Redbridge

The completed but not yet used tunnel section of the Central Line between Gants Hill and Wanstead was famously used during the Second World War as a factory to build aeroplane parts. The platforms include vertical tiled pillars and a flat roof reminiscent of the New York Subway. As you walk up the steps from the platform at Redbridge you may notice how shallow the tunnel is here. This station, unusually for a 'tube' line, was built by 'cut and cover'. Outside the station, the roundel logo shape and initials "LT" have been incorporated into the metal fence that surrounds the station – but to get there you would have walked past a 'Way out' sign and could easily miss the two roundels that are there – in reverse colours. Instead of being blue bars on a red circle, they are unusually red bars on a blue circle. Some have speculated that the red bars are meant to represent a 'red bridge' across the blue circle, to match the name of the station.

Wanstead

The plain and austere station building here was the last major work carried out for the Underground by the architects Adams, Holden & Pearson, famous for their work on Underground stations in the late-1920s and 1930s. Interesting items on the platforms include clocks with roundels on their faces in place of numbers. These also appear at neighbouring Redbridge and Gants Hill and at Bethnal Green. If you look carefully outside you will find a rare Edward VIII post box. The Village 'green' covers part of the A12 dual carriageway.

Leytonstone

Leytonstone on the west side entrance has a brilliant 'brick-work bus' statue in the middle of the bus station here. And along the corridor that is the exit/entrance to the east side of the station there is a mosaic gallery of Alfred Hitchcock films – he lived in the area for a time and this was his local station.

Leyton

Not a lot to see here. The stark facade hides an earlier building that existed when the original steam-operated line was taken over from the LNER after the Second World War. Travelling in the direction we are here, it is the last of the stations with features from its Victorian origins.

Stratford

The westbound Central Line here is one of only two points on the network (other than where trains terminate) where doors open on both sides of the platform (the other being Barking). So, if you alight from an Elizabeth Line train and are looking to exit to the south side of the station, you can board a Central Line train and exit at the opposite door to get to the other side without having to use the stairs or the lift. Another point of interest is that Stratford has the shortest escalators overall of the network – there are two of them – and they connect the southern ticket hall and Jubilee Line concourse via the mezzanine walkway.

Mile End

Mile End is very similar to the style of station that you would see on the New York subway – two island platforms, low ceilings with column supports all down the platforms and trains from two different lines either side. The thing to note here is that it's the only station on the network where 'sub-surface' lines interchange on the same level with a 'Tube' line *underground*. It happens at quite a number of other stations, but out in the open. It is the only station managed by London Underground that does not have any full-size platform name roundels.

Bethnal Green

There are two things of interest here: the clocks on the platform with roundels used on the faces instead of numerals and a plaque remembering a tragic incident in the Second World War. On the south-west corner of the junction (Roman Road entrance) you can find this above the stairs. There is also a wonderful new memorial in the park, marking the fact that 173 people died here during that war when there was a crush to enter the station during an air-raid. The journey between here and the next station calls for earplugs – it is the third noisiest stretch of track on the Underground, registering 95.2 decibels, equivalent to standing next to a power drill.

Liverpool Street

The two sub-surface platforms here are numbered 1 and 2, but go down to the Central Line and look at the signage and you'll see that the platforms are numbered 4 and 5. Platform 3 used to be a terminating platform on the sub-surface level. Go to the back of the eastbound H&C and Circle Lines platform and look out into the daylight. Across the tracks you'll see a big ugly grey building built in the spot where part of this platform and siding used to be, but most of it is still there walled off and disused.

Bank

Out of all the amazing things on the Underground that you walk past and might not notice, this might just be the best one out of all of them: find the corridor that leads down to the Waterloo & City Line. About half way down there is a large metal semi-circular ring of metal, and a plaque which tells you that this was the left-behind tunnelling shield from when the W&C Line was dug at the end of the 19th Century. It wasn't discovered until 1997, when the new corridor between the W&C Line and DLR was being built. The track in this area is sharply curved in a number of places, leading to loud screeching between the wheels and the track. When the line was built the railway company had to pay for the right to tunnel beneath properties and so followed the streets above wherever possible.

St Paul's

When escalators were introduced to this station in the 1930s a new entrance was built, and nowadays up on street level there is an odd-looking building in the middle of the triangular traffic island where King Edward Street meets Newgate Street. This is a ventilation shaft that goes down to St Paul's and is where the original station entrance/exit used to be. In those days it was named Post Office to reflect its proximity to the GPO's head office across the road.

Chancery Lane

This is the only station on the Central Line with a specially built Second World War deep level shelter beneath it, access being via the station's original entrance still in existence on the north side of High Holborn and ventilation being provided by a tower in 39 Furnival Street. For a time after the war the shelter was used as a telephone exchange.

Holborn

If travelling from Holborn to Tottenham Court Road by Central Line train, look carefully out of the right hand side windows (in the direction of travel). Visible in the gloom will be the remains of British Museum station, closed in 1933 after Holborn station had been enlarged to include platforms for the Central Line.

Tottenham Court Road

A massive redevelopment and enlargement has occurred at this station in recent years, meaning many changes have taken place. Something that has always been there at the bottom of the Central Line escalators is a circular area which is part of an old lift shaft. In the 1980s the walls were decorated with beautiful tiles by Italian artist Eduardo Paolozzi – as were the walls of the platforms too. Then, as you walk down the new widened corridor to the Central Line, see if you can spot the blocked-up passageway on the left, put in place for a connecting tunnel if Crossrail 2 is ever built. The spacious new main ticket hall is decorated by a "Diamonds and Circles" theme created by French artist Daniel Buren. See if you can find the part of the design constructed in 3D. A complete contrast is the entrance outside the Dominion theatre, which retains Art Nouveau railings dating from the early part of the 20th century.

Oxford Circus

The blue/brown/red tiles pattern of the Victoria Line is also replicated in the circular ticket hall as a nice touch of decoration to an otherwise bland area. The original Central London Railway street entrance from 1900 contrasts with the 1906 Baker Street & Waterloo Railway entrance on the other side of Argyll Street.

Bond Street

A new entrance and many lifts were installed at this station in 2017 when it was upgraded as part of the works for the Elizabeth Line. New escalators and corridors were also built, and it's along one of these corridors where you'll almost bump into something that you might not realise was there. There's a moment where one of the corridors (leading to/from the Jubilee Line) dips down and passes under a 'bump' in the ceiling. The bump is there because it's carrying the tracks of the Post Office Railway – a narrow gauge line that ran between Paddington and Whitechapel, now no longer in use.

Marble Arch

Stop and take a moment to look at the various vitreous-enam-elled panels that surround the station name roundels at plat-form level, added in the 1980s. They are some of the most colourful and delightful on the system and each design is different.

Lancaster Gate

This station was completely refurbished during 2016 with new smart, clean, white tiles. It's unusual in modern times for roundels to appear on the network with the name of the line in them, but here along the platform are small red roundels bearing the title 'Central Line'. They are modern replacements for the name friezes originally installed here in the late-1950s or early-1960s.

Queensway

One of the best shortcuts on the network is here at Queensway – it is literally less than a two-minute walk down the road from Bayswater station. If you're travelling along the Central Line and your destination is Bayswater, don't change at Notting Hill Gate.

Notting Hill Gate

Between here and Holland Park is another noisy stretch – indeed the second noisiest on the whole of the Underground, just beating Bethnal Green to Liverpool Street by 0.2 decibels (the noisiest recorded section is on the Northern Line). Like many interchange stations in central London (see also the Circle Line chapter) the station originally had no sub-surface connection for passengers on the District and Circle Lines, who had their own entirely separate station on the opposite side of the road.

Holland Park

The Central Line did of course at its eastern end once run between Epping and Ongar – it closed in 1994, but at Holland Park there is some old metal/enamel signage, where the extension to Ongar has been 'blanked over' with a white metal plate. See if you can spot where it is. For Johnston type-face aficionados, the platforms here were the first to receive its latest version – Johnston 100 – designed in 2016 in connection with the centenary of the typeface.

Shepherd's Bush

Due to the way deep-level Tube lines are laid out, it's very rare to see both running lines side-by-side in a proper Tube tunnel. Piccadilly Circus on the Bakerloo Line is still the best place to see both lines at the same time, but here is a close second. On this platform, walk all the way down to the far eastern end – furthest away from the entrance/exit – and you'll find that the platforms narrow and merge into one with some columns in the middle. The track curves sharply to the left just after trains leave this platform when travelling east.

White City

White City is one of only six 'right-hand running' stations on the network, meaning that the trains are on the 'wrong side' compared to what you would expect. Just as cars travel on the left in the UK, so do trains – except that they don't here. Like Newbury Park, this station was also awarded a prize for architectural merit during the Festival of Britain and you can still see the plaque marking this on display outside.

East Acton

For a view of the trains here at *wheel* level walk under the underpass from the entrance and come up the steps that take you to the eastbound platform, except don't go all the way. Stand about 10 steps down and wait for a train to arrive – and then leave – and you're at eye level with the wheels of a train, an unusual view and fascinating to see. A similar example is at Earl's Court on the District Line when using the spiral staircase there. The platforms here have attractive wooden waiting shelters painted in Great Western Railway colours, though are actually modern replacements.

The average speed of a train on the Underground is 20.5 miles per hour, including station stops.

North Acton

Stand on the open footbridge at North Acton, and look out for the fourth railway line that runs by here – it's for National Rail trains that occasionally run past here between London Paddington and West Ruislip. There is a once-a-day Chiltern Railways 'Parliamentary Train' service that runs along this section of line to keep the line active and avoid the long legal process required for closure.

West Acton

West Acton is a lovely example of a Grade II listed station, and on both platforms there are curved-edged waiting rooms with some nice wooden benches inside to sit on. The station looks very good lit up at night and was built in 1948 for London Transport by the Great Western Railway, its previous owner.

Ealing Broadway

Built by the Great Western Railway for Central Line trains in 1920, one of the platforms here was for many years the longest on the Underground, at 660ft.

Hanger Lane

This round station is in the middle of a roundabout with a network of subway tunnels leading to it. There is an Art on the Underground display of posters along the main tunnel leading to/from the ticket hall area, but also – if you're exiting the station ticket hall – do an immediate sharp left turn up some stairs and you'll find yourself in the middle of the busy traffic roundabout! Not a lot of people have exited this way on purpose since the gyratory road system came in of course.

Perivale

Perivale is another of the Grade II listed buildings on the Underground, and it has a nice curved canopy/frontage that is worth leaving the station and crossing the road for a good view of. It was designed and built by the Great Western Railway who owned this station – and others on the West Ruislip branch – until the Central Line took over the services in 1947 and 1948.

Greenford

Diesel trains on a service from West Ealing connect with Underground trains here. It was the last Underground station with a semaphore signal, albeit used only for Great Western trains to West Ealing. Unique is the step-free access inclined lift running between the ticket hall and the platform and worth a ride just for the experience.

Northolt

Alongside this part of the Central Line runs another railway – the 'New North Main Line' which runs from Paddington to West Ruislip and beyond. The once-a-day 'Parliamentary Train' mentioned earlier passes this station around 11.30 in the morning.

South Ruislip

The drum-shaped station building here was completed in 1960. The concrete and glass frieze in the booking hall is notable and was added to a concrete frame that had stood half-built in skeleton form since the 1940s due to lack of funds.

Ruislip Gardens

As you travel along the line towards West Ruislip, look out the left-hand side of the windows for the Central Line depot. There is also a track that spurs off to join up with the Metropolitan and Piccadilly Lines. The station itself bears witness to necessary post-Second World War cost-cutting and is very plain and basic. A grander station building was planned originally which would have had some similarities to Sudbury Hill on the Piccadilly Line. Until 1958 there were British Rail platforms here too and they were accessed via a subway from the ticket hall. Signs of where this was are still evident.

West Ruislip

Back in the 1930s when the Central Line was being extended, it was planned for there to be two more stations beyond here – *Harefield Road*, and then *Denham*. It never happened, but if you exit the Central Line at West Ruislip and cross the road to look over the bridge, you can see where the London Underground tracks would have carried on.

CIRCLE and HAMMERSMITH & CITY LINES

The Circle Line is a strange beast – never built as its own line, it was born out of two competing Underground railway companies – The Metropolitan, and Metropolitan District. They only came together and formed what was known as 'The Inner Circle' in 1884, and didn't appear on Underground maps in its own separate colour (yellow) until 1949. The Hammersmith & City Line was a section of the Metropolitan Line until it was given its own separate identity in 1990. All of its stations are shared with other lines, as is the case with the Circle Line.

Edgware Road

We'll start where Circle Line trains start: Edgware Road. On the outside of the building is the lettering 'Metropolitan Railway' for whom the station was re-built in the 1920s. The line itself is part of the original stretch of the Underground, which opened in 1863, and this and neighbouring Baker Street are the two oldest station names surviving unchanged on the Underground. The footbridge inside the station leads to staff offices on one side and a little-used entrance/exit on the other which is only open in peak hours.

Baker Street

Baker Street could probably have a whole book written just about itself! But if you're just passing through, the thing to find is the crossover passage at the western end of platforms 5 and 6 (photo above right) – almost like a forgotten passageway except that it is still in use – the original street entrance into the station would have led to here. Other features to look out for are the war memorial and WW1 shell between platforms 2 and 5. The station restaurant and buffet is now a pub and its ceiling still carries the coats of arms of the Metropolitan Railway and the places it served.

Great Portland Street

The lights hanging from the ceiling give an atmospheric feel to the station platforms, which like its neighbour at Baker Street is well worth a photo. The daylight at the western end of the platforms is a hangover from steam train days, when such openings were needed to allow out smoke and steam.

Euston Square

Everywhere on the Underground you will of course see the ubiquitous roundel – the blue bar and the red circle with the white text in the middle either saying 'Underground' or the name of the station. You'll rarely see the name of the *line* in the roundel on a station, but you can here (Holland Park is another example). Look along the platforms and you'll see old yellow and purple roundels – solid in colour with the name of the lines that Euston Square services – the Circle and the Metropolitan. They date from 1983, so there are no pink coloured ones here for the Hammersmith & City Line, which was created out of the Metropolitan in 1990 and then given its own colour.

King's Cross St Pancras

King's Cross has the greatest number of Underground lines of any station: six; two of which use the Circle Line tracks. It is one of three main line stations on the Monopoly board – the others are Liverpool Street and Marylebone. The Circle serves more main line termini than any other line, a total of nine: Euston (a short walk from Euston Square station), Paddington, Victoria, Blackfriars, Cannon Street, Fenchurch Street (a short walk from Tower Hill), Liverpool Street, King's Cross and St Pancras.

Farringdon

The station buildings on opposite sides of Cowcross Street represent a space of almost 100 years in architectural design, the Metropolitan station building dating from 1922. The name frieze below the roof shows the station's name at that time: Farringdon & High Holborn. If you exit this part of the station and turn left, on the corner of Turnmill Street you'll be able to see some further delightful old signage in ceramic.

Barbican

Barbican has a station cat! Well at least – it used to – and in memory of it there is a plaque in the ticket hall area attached to one of the supporting pillars. There are two disused platforms once used by Thameslink trains to and from Moorgate before they were diverted at Farringdon to run south.

Moorgate

Moorgate has more platforms for Underground trains than you might think, with two terminating platforms (alongside the two old Thameslink platforms) at the sub-surface platform, as well as the two normal sub-surface platforms, and the two Northern Line platforms below. There are actually *two more* platforms at this station (bringing its total to 10) which are used for the trains that start and terminate here and go up to Hertford, Stevenage and Hitchin. This line used to be part of the Underground until 1975, and it is one of London's strange 'forgotten' lines to those who do not use it on a regular basis – and there's a spiral staircase which almost no one uses to take you there.

Liverpool Street

At the west end of the eastbound platform here you will find the oldest surviving signal box on the Underground, now of course disused but retained as a listed structure. It dates from 1875.

Aldgate

For many years steam locos were changed at Aldgate and their tanks emptied. This created so much hot water and steam the local drains couldn't cope and the Metropolitan built its own sewer all the way along the Minories so the hot water could be dropped into the Thames.

Tower Hill

If you're leaving Tower Hill on a westbound train, look out of the right hand side, press your face against the glass and you might just be able to catch a glimpse of the remains of the original Tower Hill station that existed until 1967 when a new station further east replaced it. When the new station was being built a section of Roman wall was uncovered and can still be seen exposed at the east end of platform 1.

Monument

In Monument Street, around the corner from the station's Fish Street Hill entrance, there is a plaque commemorating King William Street station, the original northern terminus of the first deep-level Tube railway, the City & South London, opened in 1890. That station was later replaced by one at Bank and the 1890 line now forms part of the Northern Line.

Cannon Street

The only interesting thing that we can say about Cannon Street is that oddly it is step-free, but in the westbound direction only; only that platform has a lift.

> The line with the most stations is the District (60); the one with the fewest is the Waterloo & City (2).

Mansion House

Not the station to use if you want to visit the Mansion House – the grand building itself is opposite Bank station. It was at Mansion House station that the eastward construction of the Circle Line halted for a few years in the 1880s. The station originally had *four* platforms. One is now hidden behind a wall on the eastbound platform, and another is the former middle bay road that was removed a few years ago. Mansion House is famously one of only two stations on the Underground to have all five vowels in its name, the other being South Ealing.

Blackfriars

Blackfriars was rebuilt in 2012 and in the ticket hall area the large blue shiny tower is a huge ventilation fan, sucking out the air from down below. Note it's also possible to cross the river here by tapping in at the barrier of the National Rail station, walking the length of the platforms, and tapping out on the other side – Oyster PAYG has been programmed to let you do this and not charge you for a journey. You can thereby access Blackfriars Underground station from the south side of the river, making it the only Underground station where access is possible from either side of the Thames.

Temple

If you look along the platforms here you'll see they gently curve, making a nice pattern of pillars for a photo. Take a look at the top of these pillars – Is that a 'temple' shaped emblem in the pillars? Possibly, but at the bottom of the pillars the same symbol appears in reverse. If you have time to get out here, get a cup of tea from the café that's built into the station and then have a look at the glorious old map of the Underground that dates back to the 1930s – how the Underground map used to look before the classic Harry Beck map was introduced.

Embankment

Amongst the labyrinth of steps and escalators at Embankment is a 'green corridor'. You'll know when you find it, because it's long, flat, and has original green tiles. Walk along it, and halfway down you'll find an entrance to a spiral staircase that almost no one ever uses anymore.

Westminster

When you exit through the ticket barrier, go left, down some steps, and then right, around a bend in the corridor and you'll find the 'secret' entrance to Portcullis House – used by Members of Parliament only, this is therefore a way for them to get into the House of Commons directly from the Underground station, as there is a corridor that goes under the road linking the two buildings.

St James's Park

The headquarters of London Underground are here – above the station at 55 Broadway – housed in a magnificent 1929 building designed by Charles Holden and with sculptures by Jacob Epstein, Eric Gill and Henry Moore. On the westbound platform exactly halfway along there is some old wooden panelling where there once was a W H Smith newspaper kiosk. Meanwhile on the eastbound platform there is one roundel remaining (left here on purpose) that reads St James' Park, with no 's' after the apostrophe, evidence that the precise spelling of this station has varied over the years. See if you can spot the fake tiles which are actually metal access covers designed to blend in with the ceramic wall finishes.

> **The first dot matrix destination indicators were installed at St James's Park station in 1983.**

Sloane Square

Easily a favourite station of many Underground aficionados, get off a train and immediately look up to the daylight. You'll see two things ... the shape of arches in the brick cuttings where a glass roof used to be – destroyed by a bomb during the Second World War and never replaced. At the eastern end of the station there is a small metal fence – if you have ten minutes to spare you can exit the station, turn left, and keep going and turning left again you'll get to that fence up on street level, where you can peer over it and look down on to the station below. Then there is one of the most famous Underground facts of all – the large metal pipe that runs across the station at the western end is the river Westbourne, diverted and encased at this point when the railway was dug. The little food and drink shop midway along the westbound platform was once a pub, where you could stand on the platform and drink (and smoke!) whilst watching the trains go by.

South Kensington

Like its neighbour at Gloucester Road, South Kensington uses the old District Railway building for the entrance and exit. Abutting it is the original 1906 Piccadilly Tube building. To the east of the station, on the south side of Thurloe Square, is what is known as the 'Narrow House' squeezed in between the railway and the square – the area is so sought after that a tiny one-bed flat in this unusual house will set you back almost £1m. If you turn right after exiting the ticket barrier you will see the subway that connects the station with the local museums. It is the longest pedestrian subway link to an Underground station.

Gloucester Road

The 'car diagrams' inside the carriages of trains don't advertise Gloucester Road to be a connection between the Circle/District Lines and the deep-level Piccadilly Line, even though it is possible to do so. The route involves a fairly long flight of stairs and then going down again by lift or the much less-used spiral staircase. If you exit the station and turn right you'll find the original 1906 red brick Leslie Green Piccadilly Tube station building now converted into shops.

High Street Kensington

The majority of trains here stop at Platforms 1 and 2, but at the times when the Olympia shuttle is running trains also leave from Platform 3. Platform 3 is adjacent to Platform 2, so people often see it – but what they don't see is the fourth platform. So – at this station, see if you can find the narrow staircase that leads down to Platform 4, which trains rarely use. Then, walk up to the northern end and you'll find where the tracks from both platforms 3 and 4 were once planned to continue as part of an extension to Willesden Junction via Notting Hill Gate.

Notting Hill Gate

For a fascinating view of the sub-surface trains here, exit the station, turn right and walk around the corner until you get to Kensington Place. There is a very high wall, and you'll need to be tall. The platforms are an impressive example of the original ones along this stretch of line.

Bayswater

We admit that we're telling you something here that we have also told you about Queensway on the Central Line – the two stations are very close together. Parts of the original 1868 street level building completed when the District Railway opened are visible above the canopy. In nearby Leinster Gardens, just to the east of Bayswater, there are two dummy house frontages at 23 (shown opposite) and 24. When the properties here had to be demolished during the building of the District Railway, their facades were reinstated by the company to maintain the appearance of the street.

The last first class compartments were abolished on the Underground in October 1941, when they ceased to be available on the Metropolitan Line. They had also been available on the District Line until February 1940.

Paddington

Confusing because there are two Paddington stations; the one you want to find is the one on Praed Street, where there is a delightful red iron footbridge across the tracks that somehow feels 'in the open' despite you being underground.

Royal Oak

Is one of only five stations on the network to be named after a pub (the other four are *Angel, Elephant & Castle, Manor House and Swiss Cottage)* but the pub here is no more.

Westbourne Park

Westbourne Park appears in the 1980s pop video for Boris Gardener's "I want to wake up with you". It is one of the stations on this part of the Circle and H&C Lines to have its original street level building largely intact and is notable for its length. Its platforms have permanently displayed posters showing 'Way Out' in French and German. These are for overseas visitors to the annual Notting Hill Carnival, the nearest station, Ladbroke Grove, being closed for the duration.

Ladbroke Grove

It was at this station that the Underground's first Group Security Control Room was installed, owing to the then high crime rate on this stretch of line. It has improved since and you'll see the staff working behind the glass windows on the eastbound platform, keeping an eye on you and all the other platforms on the stretch of line via CCTV.

Latimer Road

The station here is some way from Latimer Road and is in Bramley Road. Latimer Road itself is to the north west, though it used to come further down, past the station, until the A40 extension was built.

Wood Lane

There were two older 'Wood Lane' stations near this one many years ago. When this new one was built, an old mosaic roundel from the front of the Central London Railway station a bit further south (now completely demolished) was restored and  placed at the bottom of the stairs on the westbound platform. It's beautiful and worth a look. The other Wood Lane station on this line was across the road and closer to Shepherd's Bush.

Shepherd's Bush Market and Goldhawk Road

An original station, Shepherd's Bush, used to exist between these two stations. You can walk through Shepherd's Bush market – open every day – which itself is integrated into the railway arches supporting the tracks above. Exactly halfway down in the market is where the old Underground station used to be, but sadly there's no evidence of it nowadays. TfL is the freeholder of the whole market (as it is of the market under the railway at South Harrow).

Hammersmith

This is the 'other' Hammersmith, and totally separate from the station over the road that serves the District and Piccadilly Lines. The platforms were extended a few years ago at their southern ends to allow the operation of S Stock trains. The new track of platforms 1 and 2 was built where the ticket office was and the low curved wall follows the original line of this. In contrast, the track for platform 3 now disappears from view into what was previously the train drivers' messroom.

DISTRICT LINE

The District Line came from what was originally called the Metropolitan District Railway – a competitor to the Metropolitan Railway company. It built railways in the south central part of London, with the Metropolitan in the north, until the two were forced to join up and form the Circle Line.

Ealing Broadway

A good view is possible here of the end of the line. Use the step-free ramp between platform 8 and platform 9 and there is an unusual view over the buffers. Take a moment to admire the massive train shed canopy too. The platforms here have replicas of 100 year old station name signs with solid red discs instead of rings around the name. If you go outside, look up for the name sign above the neighbouring c.1910 station building. It is now above a betting shop.

Ealing Common

In the ticketing area stop to look at the floor and admire the seven-pointed-star in the floor tiles; then look up at the patterned tiling around the area below the windows.

Acton Town

Acton Town has four platforms – the inside ones used by the Piccadilly Line and the outsides ones usually used by District Line trains (although they can be used by the Piccadilly too), but there used to be a fifth platform here as well. It was on the north side of the station, now hidden behind some advertising hoardings (right), but you can see where it used to be accessed from if you climb up the steps to the footbridge over the platforms. On the north side of the station there is a locked door, behind which used to be the walkway through to steps down to Platform 5, where you could once get a one-car shuttle service that went just one stop to South Acton.

Chiswick Park

The station here has the Piccadilly Line running non-stop on the middle two tracks. The handrails on the steps to/from the platform are painted green (to represent the District Line) with a handrail painted blue in the centre to represent the Piccadilly Line. Down in the ticketing area there are old heritage signs still in place, one of which refers to 'Mark Lane', a station renamed Tower Hill in 1946.

Turnham Green

There's nothing that special to see here, but it is worth knowing that if you're going to the actual green space that *is* Turnham Green, then Chiswick Park station is nearer.

Stamford Brook

Back in January 1964 Stamford Brook was the station chosen for the first trials of automatic ticket gates on the whole of the London Underground system. Look at the track layout to see why and note the two very contrasting styles in the two platforms – the island one was built much earlier.

Ravenscourt Park

As you enter/exit the station, there's a pretty iron grille that surrounds the main entrance. For its first eleven years as an Underground station it was called Shaftesbury Road.

Gunnersbury

There's not a lot to see at Gunnersbury. Indeed, the station entrance is hidden from view from the east by the larger commercial building into which it is incorporated. The London Overground service joins the District Line here for the service to Richmond.

Kew Gardens

Quite well-known at Kew Gardens is the pub that is on the eastbound platform (below) – in days gone by you could have walked directly onto the platform from it, but not anymore. Less well known is the footbridge to the south of the station that is Grade II listed. The railway line bisected Kew village, but it was not until 1912 that the bridge was provided to allow residents to cross the tracks safely and is a rare surviving example of a reinforced concrete structure built using a pioneering technique devised by the French engineer François Hennebique. The bridge has a narrow deck and very high walls, which once protected its users' clothing from the smoke of steam trains passing underneath. It also has protrusions on either side of the deck to deflect smoke away from the bridge structure.

Richmond

The terminus station on this branch is operated by South Western Railway. Most of the signage is therefore not in Underground style. The street entrance is of typical Southern Railway pre-war design.

Hammersmith and *Barons Court* (see Piccadilly Line)

West Kensington

Just to the east of West Kensington station lies *Ashfield House* – a TfL staff building that is used for training purposes. It is named after Lord Ashfield, chairman of the Underground Group and later London Transport between 1910 and 1947. Inside Ashfield House is a room converted into a station for training purposes, and it's called *West Ashfield* complete with a roundel. There is no public access for you to see this.

Earl's Court

The best view of the District Line at Earl's Court is if you take the walkway that goes along high up along the north side of the station and leads you to the lifts that are halfway along the platforms. Here, you get a really good view of the restored antique destination light boxes on the platforms. You can then go down the steps that would you take you to the Piccadilly Line and before going down the escalators turn around and walk through the 'mezzanine' level until you find a blocked-up door – this used to take you to a passageway that took you underneath the road and to some escalators that took visitors directly into the now closed exhibition centre. The passageway may reopen however when the giant Earl's Court housing scheme is completed. The accurate replica police phone box outside the Earl's Court Road entrance was built by apprentices at the Underground's nearby Lillie Bridge depot in 1996.

Kensington (Olympia)

This station is unique in that it has a regular service at weekends only. On Mondays to Fridays it doesn't operate unless a major exhibition is taking place. The station is however also served by London Overground trains from West Brompton, and the Olympia halls are a short walk from West Kensington station.

West Brompton

Go to the northern end of either platform, and take a look at the station name lettering. The 'W' of West Brompton crosses over, forming an interlinked 'V' type shape – you'll only see that variation in two places on the network, here and at a station on the Northern Line which we will come to later.

Fulham Broadway

The station was rebuilt in 2003 when a new shopping centre was built above the platforms and lifts were installed, but there are some old features left behind. The old footbridge (which used to lead to the old ticket hall) is still in place at the southern end of the station, and you can use it to cross platforms. By walking out of the station through the shopping centre and then turning right, 30 seconds down the road you'll find the entrance building of the old station – it's now an indoor market with places to eat and drink (see opposite). Inside there are a number of design features from the Underground still visible.

Parsons Green

If you have ever wondered whether the green referred to was once on land belonging to a Mr Parson or connected with a member of the church, the latter is the case. There has been a church and a church residence facing the green for over 600 years and the current buildings face on to the green not far south of the station.

Putney Bridge

Putney Bridge station has some unusual roundels installed on the westbound platforms that have a thin 'red edge' painted around them, unlike almost all other roundels on the network. It's also worth spotting here the additional staircases that are locked out of use – once used on Boat Race Day and for matches at the nearby Fulham Football Club. Until recently the westbound track was a dead end 'bay road' and the westbound trains used a curved platform that can still be seen in part adjacent to it.

East Putney

At East Putney, there are two standard platforms for Underground trains, but on the eastern side of the station there is a gently-curved *third* platform. Interestingly, this isn't used for Underground trains, but instead is a piece of track that connects up to the National Rail network, and trains from the South Western Railway sometimes pass through here to go to and from the depot at Wimbledon Park. There are also a couple of scheduled passenger trains which come this way early in the morning and late at night but don't stop.

Southfields

The best time to see Southfields is when the Wimbledon tennis championships are on. This station is the nearest Underground station to the grounds and the platforms are often covered with imitation grass and other tennis-themed decorations during this period.

Wimbledon Park

This station and the neighbouring Southfields in similar style were built in 1889, and many original parts of the building remain, but part of the entrance here is now a small shop. At one time, during the tennis tournament, British Rail attached additional notices to the platform name signs stating: "Alight at next stop for Wimbledon tennis" and this was always true, because whichever direction you were travelling in, the next station was served by the special bus service.

Wimbledon

In common with Richmond, this station is operated by South Western Railways. It is unique as an Underground station in having interchange with trams.

Gloucester Road to Tower Hill – See Circle Line

Aldgate East

Aldgate East station today is not where it was when the line was built. The original 1884 station was moved in 1938, and in the process the existing track was lowered by two metres, whilst keeping the track open during the day for running trains. The bed underneath the track was excavated, and the track held up by a timber trestle work. Once excavation was complete and the new station constructed around the site, construction workers then lowered the whole track in one night. The track was lowered using ropes threaded through round metal brackets fitted to the ceiling and these can still be seen in place. Note also the occasional patterned tiles placed randomly on the walls and see if you can find one depicting the Crystal Palace; this building burned down two years before the station opened. The station's eastern entrance is incorporated within the Whitechapel Art Gallery.

Whitechapel

The station used to have four platforms at surface level, but has been massively rebuilt to incorporate the Elizabeth Line. Though no longer visible from the platforms, the Overground service passes under the Underground here.

Stepney Green

In the entrance (just after the barriers) on the way into the station, there is a very old style of sign here that says 'To The Trains' complete with hand/finger graphic.

Mile End (See Central Line)

Bow Road and Bromley-by-Bow

One of the steepest gradients overall of the network is on this section of the Underground – the incline here is 1:28.

West Ham

West Ham, which until 1999 was served by only one other rail service, now has three others: c2c into Fenchurch Street, the Jubilee Line and the Docklands Light Railway, making it an important interchange set in a low-density residential area.

Plaistow

The old ticket hall is delightful and is subject to a local listing. See if you can spot the old 'Ticket Office' sign.

Upton Park

You might think West Ham Underground would have been closest to the old West Ham football stadium. But no, for the football club it was Upton Park station. For some time after the football club moved to the Olympic Stadium, the signs at Upton Park saying 'West Ham F.C. this way' were still up.

East Ham

East Ham is a fairly nondescript Victorian station built by the London, Tilbury & Southend Railway, but there is something delightful to spot here. Go onto the westbound platform and about half way look up on the corner of the brick wall and you can see the hand-painted sign that says 'Tea 2D a cup' that has been there many, many, years.

Barking

This station is managed by railway operator c2c and also hosts London Overground trains terminating on the service from Gospel Oak. The subways and the long sloping ramps that link them were provided for parcels traffic. Eastbound District Line trains open their doors on both sides here.

Upney and Becontree

At Becontree, at the western end of the station, note that the platforms used to be much longer – they are now disused and slightly overgrown. British Railways used to stop services here (with longer trains) but ceased in 1962.

Dagenham Heathway, Dagenham East and Elm Park

Out on the eastern end of the District Line several stations have taken to playing classical music over the PA in the evening, as it has proved to be a useful deterrent to youths loitering at stations who find the idea of listening to such music intolerable.

> The first female Underground train driver began driving on the District Line in 1978.

Hornchurch

There are old platforms to the side of the present-day ones, now overgrown and whose foliage blows in the draught caused by the passing of the now non-stopping main line Rail trains that would have once called here.

Upminster Bridge

The brown and cream tiles in the floor of the booking hall are that of a 'swastika' pattern, and as might be expected, date from before the Second World War. Another oddity is that it is the only station on the Underground to have a red phone box kiosk inside it. This was installed after the original varnished wood callbox had to be removed to comply with modern fire regulations.

Upminster

Upminster is another of the small number of stations on the Underground not owned or managed by TfL, which is why none of the station signs here are of the classic roundel. There is one roundel here though, at the eastern end of platform 5 you'll see one on the side of the signal box which controls the District Line trains coming into the station. And there's the lovely old antique 'Next train' lightbox indicator on the footbridge here too.

JUBILEE LINE

The Jubilee Line was originally built to provide relief to the central area of the Bakerloo Line. Intended to be called 'The Fleet Line', it was renamed by order of the Greater London Council to mark the Queen's Jubilee in 1977 – only that it ended up opening two years later in 1979. At first the line ran between Stanmore (at the end of a former Bakerloo Line branch) and Charing Cross, but in the late-1990s it was extended through the new development at Canary Wharf and then to Stratford. A small 'stub' that ran from Green Park to Charing Cross became disused.

Stanmore

On the steps down to the platforms is a display of Art on the Underground posters. Or – for a unique way to get into (or out of) the station – go via the car park, which is the step-free entrance, that takes you down a long gentle sloping path which leads you into the station via a way that you might not normally realise was there. Whilst you're here, look at the brand-new waiting room on the new Platform 3 – no one ever uses it as people immediately board the train, so it seems a bit pointless that it's been built there.

Canons Park

There is a good view to be had here of Wembley Stadium. Indeed if the line were to continue perfectly straight, it would take you into the stadium.

Queensbury and Kingsbury

Queensbury was not a pre-existing name but was chosen because it would fit nicely with its adjacent station on the line, Kingsbury. Step outside Queensbury station and there's a large roundabout dominated in the middle by a fantastic 'UNDERGROUND' logo.

Wembley Park (see Metropolitan Line)

Neasden, Dollis Hill, Willesden Green and *Kilburn*

All the stations on this stretch of the Jubilee Line run along-side the Metropolitan Line, so you'll note that some stations have disused platforms each side where many years ago Metropolitan Line trains used to stop. With some small exceptions they have run through non-stop since the service to these stations was taken over by the Bakerloo Line in 1939 (and the Jubilee Line forty years later). At Kilburn there is a nice bridge outside the station, painted light blue and deep purple and with the name 'METROPOLITAN RAILWAY' along with the date it was installed.

West Hampstead

If you're heading north from this station, it can often be quicker to take a train one stop south, change at Finchley Road and board a northbound Metropolitan Line train instead. West Hampstead has three railway stations serving different lines that are all close together and there have been proposals to connect them in some way, with added stops on the Chiltern and Metropolitan lines giving a five-line hub. Nothing definite is planned at the moment, but this is the closest three stations of three different lines come to each other in London.

Finchley Road (See Metropolitan Line)

Swiss Cottage

The dark-wood coloured escalators are a joy to see here, as is the 'Way out' uplighter in roundel form that you can see here as well. So, jump off the train here, go for a ride up the escalators and admire them. Like Aldgate East, there are occasional patterned tiles here carrying designs relating to London and the Home Counties.

St John's Wood

This is the London Underground station to go to if you want Abbey Road (the famous recording studios used by The Beatles) ... which is confusing because there is a stop on the DLR in East London called 'Abbey Road'. Just outside the station there is a Beatles-themed coffee shop. The station does have an apostrophe in its name on the outside of the station, on the Underground map, and on carriage maps inside Jubilee Line trains, but the roundels on the platform of the station itself omit these. They date from 1939 and LT only started adding apostrophes to its signs in the 1950s. This is another station where you can play "spot the patterned tile".

Baker Street, *Bond Street* and *Green Park*

These three stations have a common style that dates from the time the line opened in 1979. Just after leaving Green Park the original tunnel that took the line to its original southern terminus of Charing Cross can be seen from the train. Look out on the same side as the platform; the tunnel can be made out by the gap in the tunnel cabling.

Westminster

This is arguably the most magnificent station on the Jubilee Line extension – perhaps on all of the Underground in the modern era. Take rides on the escalators – up and down – that take you to the Jubilee Line platforms and wonder about the complexity of engineering that went into building this station – including supporting the nearby Big Ben Tower to stop it leaning over. Once done, the thing to find here is the secret entrance into Portcullis House – a government building that only employees can use to enter/exit the station. Exit through the barriers, turn left, down some steps, and then follow a passageway to the right that takes you under the road – just here there are some brown coloured revolving doors that are the 'secret' way in!

Waterloo

The elephant in the room – well, at the top of the escalators built for the Jubilee Line. The elephant originally appeared on the Underground as part of a temporary art display at Gloucester Road, but was moved to where it is now as there was a permanent space available. The station is  next to where stood what is usually credited as the world's first circus arena.

Southwark

At the top of the escalators you'd normally turn left to exit the station via the regular ticket office area. But if you instead turn right and go up a lesser used escalator, you'll find yourself in an odd area: a gateline for the Underground, a few metres after which there is nothing but another gateline – which is for Waterloo East station which is now above you! It's a "no man's land" between the two gatelines but you will not be charged for crossing it.

London Bridge

Joiner Street, a name that remains, was permanently closed for the Jubilee Line extension to give a better interchange between London Bridge tube and the main line station.

Bermondsey

When the Jubilee Line extension was being built, huge efforts were put into the design of these stations to make each unique. Here at Bermondsey, it's been built in such a way that even though it's deep underground, natural daylight still comes in and partly lights up the platforms below.

Canada Water

The wide island Jubilee platforms here enable both eastbound and westbound sides of it to be used for peak traffic in one direction. There is a similar one at the next station, Canary Wharf. The station once had all of its signs changed to "Buxton Water" for a day as part of an advertising stunt.

Canary Wharf

This enormous station, the only London tube station to be designed by Sir Norman Foster, was built in a disused dock and has the widest 'island' platform on the whole system at 17.2 metres (photo opposite).

Oyster was introduced in 2003.
Other names considered for the
ticketing system before its
launch included Pulse and Gem.
The Oyster name was registered
by a private company (Transys)
with whom TfL later fell out. It
had to buy the name from them
in 2010 at a reported cost of £1m.

North Greenwich

A moment can be taken to stop and look and think how much work went into excavating North Greenwich to build the station underground. Its first major role was as the station serving the Millennium Dome, now the O2 Arena. The layout of the platform and tracks here allowed for a possible future extension towards Thamesmead, but this is not likely to occur in the foreseeable future, if at all.

Canning Town

The Jubilee Line comes into the open just before it reaches Canning Town station and runs alongside the Docklands Light Railway to just south of Stratford station. Both are on the alignment of a disused main line service. Canning Town has a design that takes into account the need to support the Beckton branch of the Docklands Light Railway which runs directly above it; the only case where a DLR station occupies the space immediately above an Underground station. There are some fake owls in the station's booking area to deter pigeons; uniquely the station roundels here have spikes on them for the same purpose.

West Ham

Now an important interchange with other lines, many more people change trains here than exit or enter the station. The platform is in a plain but attractive red brick design.

Stratford

The largest interchange station outside central London, the Jubilee terminates here and connects with the Central Line, the Elizabeth Line, the Overground, two branches of the DLR and a number of main line services between Liverpool Street and Essex and East Anglia.

The Jubilee Line is the only line on the Underground to have platform edge doors at some of its stations.

METROPOLITAN LINE

The Metropolitan Line is the daddy of all Underground lines. It started as the Metropolitan Railway company and London's first underground railway had seven stations from Paddington to Farringdon. It soon expanded out into the suburbs, "Metroland", with its first director having grand plans to expand much further. Today, we know it as the Metropolitan Line.

Amersham

If you stand on the footbridge that straddles the station, you are at the highest possible point that you can be on the Underground system, as Amersham station is 150 metres above sea level. It's not the most western station though – that falls to Chesham – but the sidings in the distance where trains reverse make the difference. Passengers aren't allowed to this part, but when the drivers go there they are then at the most westerly part of the Underground network. This and the next four stations are among five Underground stations outside the boundary of the M25 (the other one being Epping on the Central Line).

Chesham

Chesham is a delightfully cute station – with hints of how it used to be bigger – an abandoned platform (now a garden which has won an award), the old signal box and water tower are still here – unused – on this now simple single platform station. As you travel back from here to Chalfont & Latimer it takes a long time, as at 3.9 miles it is the longest stretch of track between two consecutive stations on the network.

Chalfont & Latimer

A four-car shuttle train used to run between here and Chesham many years ago, which is why there is now a disused platform 3 at Chalfont station. It could not be used when new

'S Stock' trains were introduced in 2012 as they were all of a fixed eight cars in length.

Chorleywood

When this station originally opened in 1889, it was known as "Chorley Wood" and was then called "Chorley Wood and Chenies" for a time. A lot of the original station features remain – a favourite is on the southbound platform: it is an immense pleasure to go and sit inside the waiting room and soak up the atmosphere of days gone by with its gorgeous red wooden benches. On the northbound platform there is a disused signal box which was recently restored and painted in Metropolitan Railway colours.

Rickmansworth

There is a water tower at the north end of the southbound platform which gives a clue as to what used to happen here – steam trains. Rickmansworth was once the changeover point between electric- and steam-hauled trains when both were still running up to 1961. There is also a remaining disused platform at the eastern end of the southbound platform with rusty rails, and where no train has been for many years.

Moor Park

If you've travelled south from Rickmansworth to get here, then have a look out the left-hand window, and you'll see some track disappearing around a bend which is known as the 'North Curve'. This track allows trains to get onto the Watford branch without going down to Moor Park. There are just one or two trains a day that travel over this stretch of track.

Croxley

On the stairwell down to the northbound platform the staff here do an excellent job of maintaining a gallery of photos from days-gone-by on the Metropolitan Line. "Steam on the Met" photos also feature heavily – these are of the heritage services that have occasionally run on the Metropolitan Line.

Watford

Watford is under threat from closure. There are plans to extend the Metropolitan Line just after Croxley to Watford

The London Underground map came second in a 2006 BBC competition to find viewers' favourite British design of the 20th Century. The magazine Time Out placed it at number 1 in its view in 2013. TfL's own Design Icons competition that same year found it at number 3.

Junction, which would see this station close, but the plans keep getting pushed back on finance grounds. Watford is a very quiet station compared with its neighbour at the Junction and the Metropolitan Railway had always wanted to get to the centre of the town, but without success.

Northwood

At the delightful Northwood station (used as the station that you'll see in the 1970s BBC sitcom *The Good Life)* check out the 'porthole' style round window at the top of the footbridge that lets you look down onto the tracks below.

Northwood Hills

This might just be the first 'bland' station on the Metropolitan Line as you head south! There's not much to see here, but there is a delightful fact – the name 'Northwood Hills' was chosen from a reader's suggestion in a local newspaper competition of what to name the station, but it is actually *lower* than its adjacent station – Northwood.

Pinner

For many years until the 1960s this suburban Metro-land station was also served by Great Central main line trains to Manchester and Sheffield. They reached it from Marylebone via Harrow-on-the-Hill.

The first baby was born on the Underground in 1924 at Elephant & Castle. Four others have been born on the system since, two of them at Liverpool Street.

North Harrow

This station is the last on the Met to retain the original wooden shelters from when it opened as a quiet 'halt' in open countryside in 1913. There is also an original stencilled station name above the disused east-facing entrance.

Harrow-on-the-Hill

Harrow-on-the-Hill has a lot of signage that hasn't been replaced and updated in quite some time, many of the line diagrams are very old – for example on platforms 3 and 4, there is a sign that shows the service to Chesham as still being a shuttle, rather than the 'through' service that it is now. Also, note that on the signs on the platforms that show the platform numbers, there is a faint roundel depicted in the background too, a lovely little attention to detail that is often missed by the commuter in a hurry. If you use the subway that links all six platforms you can see where the goods lifts were that were used for mail and parcels.

Northwick Park

It's not shown on a Underground map – but perhaps it really should be – that is, a connector blob between Northwick Park and Kenton station on the Bakerloo Line, because they are very close together and can be walked between in about five minutes.

Preston Road

Go one stop more though, and at Preston Road the current day station platforms are located to the west side of the road bridge – but they were not originally. Look over the wall on the bridge to the *east* and you can see where the original station used to be and also the remains of a second world war air raid shelter.

Wembley Park

This station is another of those with plastic owls. Why? To deter pigeons and the mess they leave behind. They can be found in the modern booking hall, which gets very busy when there is an event on at Wembley Stadium.

Finchley Road

Between here and Baker Street, the first daylight stretch is a former station at Marlborough Road. The station building itself is still in existence and is currently in use as a substation. There was also a Lords station after this, for the cricket ground, but not much is visible of it these days.

Baker Street

On top of Baker Street station is a block of 180 flats known as Chiltern Court. This block was completed in 1929 for the Metropolitan Railway and is the largest residential block above an Underground Station.

Great Portland Street to Aldgate (See Circle Line)

West Harrow

An unusual station on the Underground in that if you were to change directions here you must exit to the street and walk under the bridge at street level to get to the entrance for the other side.

Rayners Lane

The area around these two stations was just farmland when they were first built – the local farmer was a Mr Rayner after whom the 'lane' and then the station was named.

Eastcote

The platforms at Eastcote have some large flowerbeds and grow some of the best flowers that you'll see at any station on the network.

Ruislip Manor

In the ticket hall there's a brilliant old clock high up on the wall that is unlike anything you'll see at any other Underground station on the network.

Ruislip

The distance between Ruislip and Ruislip Manor is very short – it takes just one minute to travel between the two stations. And look out for the delightful old signal box at the eastern end of Ruislip station.

Ickenham

The original 1905 electrical sub-station is still in use today and can be seen adjacent to the eastbound track beyond Glebe Avenue. The platforms are delightfully walled in greenery in a remarkable contrast with the next station on the line, which is more like a greenhouse.

Hillingdon

The station was paid for out of the roads budget. It had to be re-sited from its original location when the A40 road was widened here. The station was in the way, so had to move. When it was, a magnificent glass station with a glazed passageway from the street was built to replace the old one, all paid for out of the roads budget. Sadly it is looking the worse for wear at present. On the new railway bridge over the road the 'roundel' shape has been used in the bricks that make up its walls.

Uxbridge

Easily one of the most decorative and splendid stations on the Metropolitan Line, when you're not marvelling at the general impressiveness of this design classic by famed Underground architect Charles Holden, look out for the weighing machines on the platform, the beautiful old 'Buffet' sign in the ticket hall area, the stained glass windows which light up on a sunny day, the preserved cigarette vending machines right by the entrance, or step outside and look up – way up – above the main entrance, to see two beautiful wings on wheels sculptures by Joseph Armitage.

NORTHERN LINE

The Northern Line was built as two separate railway companies (the 'Hampstead Tube' and the City & South London Railway) which merged to form what is now the Northern Line. The two branches through the centre of London are a result of this amalgamation. The line has more stations south of the Thames than any other Underground line and prior to 1937 it was called the Morden-Edgware Line. It received its seemingly unsuitable current name when former Great Northern Railway branches north of Highgate were being taken over.

Morden

Morden was the UK pioneer of 'park and ride' when it opened in 1926, a garage being provided by the Underground opposite the station. Before you enter the station, cross the busy road outside the station and find the bridge where you can look south and see the trains coming in and out of the depot south of Morden station. Once you are ready to start your journey, inside the station look up high to see if you can spot the plastic owl, and then look for the mural on disused Platform 1 as well the plants growing as part of the station garden.

South Wimbledon

On the southbound platform there is a name sign that still says 'South Wimbledon [Merton]' on it – it's the only one left. This sub-title is more accurate as the station is certainly in Merton. Railway companies often used the name of a better known nearby town and just added a compass point.

Colliers Wood

Exit the station, cross over the road, and you'll find that the local pub is called 'The Charles Holden'. Holden was the revered architect who designed many London Underground stations, including all of those south of Stockwell on this stretch of the Northern Line when the line was extended in the 1920s. The pub has local history photos on its walls, including the station.

Tooting Broadway and Tooting Bec

Two excellent Charles Holden stations. Tooting Bec has an unusual exit 'island' as one of its exits as it pops up at various places on the surface. Tooting Broadway in particular looks great from a distance across the road when lit up at night. It was used with the opening credits of the TV series 'Citizen Smith'.

Balham

A bomb exploded here in the street outside during World War II, and the road collapsed into the Underground station below the street killing people who were sheltering there. There used to be just a simple plaque commemorating this in the ticket hall area, but now it's been expanded with several old photos, more information and is more like a museum display. It is worth seeing and reading.

Clapham South

Clapham South is one of seven locations on the Northern Line where additional tunnels were built – deep-level shelters that are *below* the Underground stations – and used by people to shelter in during the Second World War. Exit the station at Clapham South, cross over onto the common and immediately you'll see a round 'pill box' shaped building. This is the northern entrance with a spiral staircase inside that leads down to the shelters (see photos on next page). There is an information board here set up by *Subterranea Britannica* with more information. There used to be a way in to the shelter from the Underground station platforms – but it's now been blocked up. Can you work out where it used to be?

Clapham Common

There's a design classic at Clapham Common station with its delightful domed roof. Exit the station (noting the brilliant 'To the Trains' sign as you do) cross over the street and look back to admire it fully. It is not the original 1900 station though, being built in the 1920s. Kennington has a similar one, though the one here dates from its opening in 1890.

Clapham North

At both Clapham North and Clapham Common there is a narrow island platform – 14 feet in width – these are now the only two deep tube stations on the Underground with narrow platforms like this serving both directions, but there were two others – at Angel and Euston – until they were upgraded.

Stockwell

The very first journey on an electric tube railway began from Stockwell on 4th November 1890. With the Prince of Wales on board it was also the first royal journey on an Underground train. The journey from here to its City terminus at King William Street (near the Monument) took 18 minutes. Today, the platforms here are in a unique decor for the southern section of the Northern Line. They were modernised in the early 1970s in similar style to the new Victoria Line.

Oval

Exit the station (if you're feeling fit) by walking up the spiral staircase, but whereas the sign says there are 80 steps you'll find that there are 103. When you get to the top, you'll see the cricket murals on the wall and even a book swap shelf.

Kennington

Kennington also has a rare domed roof like Clapham Common station, but many people never see this one as it is where lots of people just change trains between the two different branches. Trains off the Charing Cross branch terminate here, and you have to cross platforms to carry on going south to Morden – but have you ever wondered where the trains go? Well, wonder no more ... as it's perfectly possible to *stay on* a terminating train and when you do, the train goes around a little known loop of track, and comes back into Kennington station on the northbound branch heading up to Charing Cross. This 'loop' has now been broken into and used as part of the Northern Line Extension to Battersea Power Station.

Nine Elms and *Battersea Power Station*

As this is being written in advance of these two stations opening, we don't have the clairvoyance to know what things to look for here! Battersea Power Station station will be the only station on the Underground with 'station' in its name, unless it gets renamed before opening.

Waterloo and *Embankment*

When this section of the Northern Line was first dug, the line used to terminate at Embankment, and similar to the 'Kennington Loop' there was a section of 'looped' line here that turned a southbound train around, and came back into service as a northbound one. The loop goes right underneath the River Thames and is still there today – sealed up, after a section of it flooded during World War II when a bomb damaged the roof of the tunnel. Evidence that it is here can be seen if you look at the perfectly straight Northern Line southbound platform, then go to the northbound platform to see that it is curved because it was built on a section of the loop.

Charing Cross

A lot of TV and movie filming takes place at Charing Cross – the sequence in James Bond's 'Skyfall' took place here on the disused escalators that go down to the now also disused

Jubilee Line platforms here. The name shown in the film was Temple; a District and Circle Lines station and completely wrong for a deep-level Tube. There's also a ventilation shaft – access to which is via a black gate along a corridor off the Northern Line – used in an episode of TV's 'Sherlock'.

Leicester Square

Here are two other design features on the Underground that many people walk past without noticing. As you walk up the steps to the exits look again, and you'll see in the tiles the letters 'LT' have been engraved on the walls all the way down (LT for 'London Transport'). On the original Leslie Green station (red building) for the Piccadilly Line station there is evidence of offices above it being originally used by the publishers of the Wisden Cricketers' Almanac. An image of cricket stumps appears in the tilework above a doorway.

Tottenham Court Road

As on the Central Line, the platforms on the Northern have some surviving tiles of Eduardo Paolozzi's artwork from the 1980s, great to stop and admire instead of rushing onto your next train.

Goodge Street

If you exit the station here, cross the road and enter Chenies Street a little to the south. Fifty metres down, you'll find the Eisenhower Centre – entrance to another of the Second World War deep-level Tube shelters and now used for document storage.

Warren Street

Here is one of the small number of stations that still has old tiles at platform level revealing the original name. Go to the back end of the southbound platform here, and you'll see that the station's original name *Euston Road* is still shown.

Euston

The southbound City branch platform is wider than you will normally see on the tube lines. This is because until the late 1960s, the Northern Line here had a narrow island platform similar to those still in existence at Clapham North and Clapham Common. It was widened when the Victoria Line was built and new platform tunnels provided for that line and for the northbound Northern.

King's Cross St Pancras

At the foot of the escalators to the two Northern Line platforms is a piece of artwork easily missed. It is one half of a two part work, the other being on the Piccadilly Line here. Named 'Full Circle', it is described in official publicity as an item that is 'almost incognito yet remains elegantly obvious'. Maybe you use the Northern Line at this station regularly. Have you noticed it?

Angel

It's probably one of the most well-known facts about the Underground system; that Angel has the longest escalator on the whole of the system – it takes a full minute and a half if you stand still on it. It's here, because (like Euston) the station used to have a narrow island platform and then lifts to the surface, but it was massively reconstructed during the 1990s with the escalators and a new entrance. If you exit the current station, turn left and walk around the corner to Torrens Street, you can see the old station building, now abandoned and disused – but quite clearly still recognisable as part of the Underground. In order to replace the old narrow platform, a new northbound line and platform was constructed, meanwhile the southbound platform was widened by taking over the space where the original north-bound track was. Compare the widths of the two platforms today and you'll realise how this was done.

Old Street

Old Street has connecting corridors to the service from Moorgate, which until 1975 was part of the tube. You may have arrived at Old Street many times on the Northern Line and never gone to the other line that comes here – but if you do it feels a little like you're stepping back in time to a little known part of the railway network in London.

Bank (See Central Line)

London Bridge (See Jubilee Line)

Borough

See if you can find the plaque at the station (in the ticket hall area, often overlooked) which mentions how parts of disused tunnels here were adapted to public air-raid shelters that were used between 1940 and 1945.

Elephant & Castle (See Bakerloo Line)

Mornington Crescent

You can't mention Mornington Crescent without mentioning the BBC Radio 4 quiz "I'm sorry I haven't a clue", the spoof-quiz game where the rules were made up and anything could happen until one of the players announced: 'Mornington Crescent' to win the game. One of the long-time hosts of the programme was Willie Rushton – now sadly passed – and there is a blue plaque tribute to him in the ticket office area here. Also, Mornington Crescent unusually has an abandoned emergency staircase. The station was closed for an extended period in the 1990s and when it was rebuilt, a new staircase was put in, leaving the original old spiral staircase hidden away behind a blue grilled door.

Camden Town

Camden Town is a really congested station, and TfL know it! For twenty years or more the Underground has been attempting to rebuild it. The latest plan is to have another entrance/exit to ease congestion. In the meantime, the congestion is why a connector to Camden Road station on the Overground, a short walk up the road, doesn't appear on the Underground map – as TfL do not want to encourage people to make that connection! If you do find yourself at Camden Town changing from one Northern Line branch to another, you can use the lesser-used passageway at the southern end of the station to connect to all platforms; it's usually less busy than the corridors at the bottom of the escalators.

> During the height of the Blitz in the second world war around 180,000 people sheltered on tube platforms.

Edgware

Go to the northern ends of any of the platforms here, look closely at the roundels. The 'W' in Edgware crosses over at the top, forming a small 'V' type shape – you'll only see that on the network in two places, here and as mentioned earlier at a station on the District Line.

Burnt Oak to *Brent Cross*

Burnt Oak, Hendon Central and Brent Cross share the distinction on the Underground of having a chessboard pattern on the floors of their booking halls. Burnt Oak had the suffix Watling when it first opened and two roundels on the platform here still show this. Hendon Central and Brent Cross both have an impressive Doric colonnade at the front.

Golders Green

Golders Green station has a platform that passengers can't get on to. There are four platforms in public use here, but they're numbered 2 to 5. Look over at platform 1 and if there's anyone on it, it will be a Train Operator waiting to take over a train. Platform 1 is only ever used by train crew – there's even a vending machine installed on it for their benefit.

Hampstead

One to remember for pub quizzes again – Hampstead is the deepest station on the network in terms of how far underground it is from street level. There is another clue here also to a station name once planned or used: there is lettering in the tilework that says 'Heath Street' – a name that the station was going to be called before it opened as Hampstead. As the deepest station on the network, there are 320 steps on the spiral staircase here, and there's a rumour that going back for many years, the Station Supervisor here has kept a log book and in it are listed many recorded times for ascending the stairs. Apparently, whenever a new member of staff turns up to work at the station, they are made to walk the whole station for familiarisation purpose – and that includes the very long staircase. When they do walk up it, they are timed to see how long they take.

Belsize Park

As per other Northern Line stations that we've mentioned (Clapham South, Goodge Street) Belsize Park is one of seven locations on the Northern Line where a wartime deep-level shelter was built. Exit the station to see the two circular-shaped buildings that are the entrances to these secret shelters a little way down the hill. One is on Haverstock Hill down an alley by a parade of shops; the other is on the corner of Downside Crescent.

Chalk Farm

Chalk Farm has the shallowest lifts on the Northern Line. It is usually quicker to use the steps (there are 53 of them) than wait for the lift. And if you're a music fan – or even if you are not – take a moment to admire the Leslie Green frontage of this station. It was used on the cover of 'Absolutely' – a 1980s album by the band *Madness*.

High Barnet

To enable step-free access at this station, there is a path and ramp which takes you around the north end of the station and is great for a look back down at the trains from the buffers. The 'branch line' architecture that survives is typical of many stations on the High Barnet line, which was originally opened by the Great Northern Railway in 1872.

Totteridge & Whetstone and Woodside Park

Totteridge & Whetstone has the distinction of having the greatest number of characters in its name (20 if you count the ampersand) on the Underground. It is not however the longest name on the Underground map, for this is an honour that goes to 'Cutty Sark for Maritime Greenwich' – a DLR station. It is a rather bland station and the platforms often feel like a sleepy branch line with nothing much interesting to look at. However, just one stop further towards London is Woodside Park, which is a delightful station with lots of old and original features.

West Finchley

The way in and out of this station is on the northbound side, and there is then a footbridge over to the southbound side. But! Walk to the far southern end of the southbound platform and there is a locked gate. You can only unlock it if you have a *RADAR* key, used by those with accessibility issues – this is a step-free entrance primarily for use by those in wheelchairs.

The station was only opened in 1933, and due to a shortage of funds, the station buildings and footbridge were salvaged from other parts of the LNER system.

Mill Hill East

The line used to go farther here back in the days of LNER steam – all the way to Edgware, and if you exit the station and turn left, walk up the street for about a minute and you'll find a path/trail on the left that you can walk along which follows the path of the old abandoned railway line. It had been planned to extend the Northern Line along it, but the Second World War postponed it and scaling back after the war cancelled it. The line got as far as Mill Hill East only because of the army barracks that existed opposite the station. The land on which these were sited is now used for housing.

Finchley Central

Henry (Harry) Beck – who designed the classic Underground map – used to live in Finchley and this was one of his local stations. On the southbound platform you'll find a plaque and a reproduction of his original 1933 Underground map.

East Finchley

From the southern end of the platforms, look up and you'll see 'The Archer' – a 3-metre tall statue by artist Eric Aumonier, the statue supposedly firing its arrow into the 17 mile-long tunnel section that doesn't emerge into daylight again until you get all the way down to Morden. It's a delight to see and fits in well with the original waiting rooms and other features on the platforms. The tracks in the middle here are rarely used for 'in service' passenger trains as they come to/from a nearby depot.

Highgate

As part of aborted plans to expand the Northern Line in the late-1930s there are the remnants of a station above ground here as well as underground. The island platform can be seen through the bushes from Archway Road. The line would have gone to Alexandra Palace via Muswell Hill, along the route of which there is now a woodland walk. The Underground platforms at Highgate are longer and were designed to accommodate trains of nine carriages in length. A few such trains ran as a trial shortly before the war, but the idea was not pursued.

Archway

This station was originally called Highgate and was where the line terminated when it was first built. When the Northern Line expanded and the station that we now know as Highgate was built, this station became 'Archway' – another local name – and if you look along at platform level, you'll see there are decorative black metal arches.

Tufnell Park

Tufnell Park is one of the lesser-used stations along this branch of the Northern Line. It's used as a local commuter station, but in the middle of the day it can be eerily quiet – so quiet in fact, that people have been known to post fake videos onto the internet claiming it to be an 'abandoned station'.

Kentish Town

Before TfL took over London Underground a non-LT railway used to appear on the Underground map – that being the Thameslink line from Kentish Town down through the City to Elephant & Castle and beyond. TfL now show only their services on the Underground map. It's often quicker though to make this journey by not going on the Underground. Check the times of the southbound Thameslink trains from Kentish Town, and you may just find that your journey is faster.

PICCADILLY LINE

The Piccadilly Line started out as the Great Northern, Piccadilly & Brompton Railway running from Finsbury Park through central London to Hammersmith with a 'stub' off to Aldwych where there had originally been plans to run south under the river. In the 1930s the line was extended at both ends with many stations being designed by architect Charles Holden. It also has the greatest number of abandoned stations (six) on the network, making it rich with history. We will start in the west from Heathrow.

Heathrow Terminal Stations

A lesser known fact about the Heathrow Underground stations is that you can travel between them *free*. You still must tap in with an Oyster or Contactless card, but if you travel between any of the three Heathrow Underground stations, you won't be charged anything – this is to allow people at the airport to make connections between the different airport terminals without charge. Heathrow Terminal 4 is just one of four stations on the Underground to have just one platform – Chesham, Mill Hill East, and Kensington (Olympia) are the others. The station at Heathrow Terminal 5 is not owned by the Underground but by airport operator BAA as an integral part of their Terminal 5 building.

Hatton Cross

On the platform can be found enamel panels that have reference to the British Airways *Speedbird* logo of the 1970s. Up at ticket hall level look at the wrought iron hanging basket holders and the London Underground symbol that has been shaped in them. When this station opened in 1975 there were 279 stations on the Underground, a total that has never been exceeded. Since that time, two complete lines have been lost: the Northern City Line in 1975, when it closed for the service to transfer to BR, and the East London Line, which closed in 2007 to be absorbed into London Overground.

Hounslow West

When Charles Holden designed the stations on the western extension of the Piccadilly, he did so with artistic flourish. Get out at Hounslow West and walk up to the ticket hall and look up at the ceiling to see how splendid it looks. The line used to end directly behind this building until the Piccadilly was extended to Heathrow airport via new tunnelling in the 1970s.

Hounslow Central and Hounslow East

If you're outside the station at Hounslow East, admire the large green sloping roof … and if you're outside the station at Hounslow Central, there are some preserved 'London Transport' signs, a name that hasn't been used since 2000 when TfL took over.

Osterley

As you leave the station heading east, look out of the window and a few seconds later you will see the abandoned platforms of the previous Osterley station, then known as 'Osterley & Spring Grove'. The old street building is currently a bookshop, and if you go inside you can still find the windows (now blocked up) of the old ticket office.

Boston Manor

Another Charles Holden masterpiece. Lit up at night, it has appeared in posters and also on one of the stamps issued by Royal Mail in 2013 to commemorate the 150th anniversary of the Underground. Note how the pillars on the platform at this station are painted black and gold – perhaps a nod towards nearby Brentford football club, whose nickname is 'The Bees'.

Northfields

Northfields station once had two exits, and on the platforms the 'Way Out' signs unusually give the name of the road outside. The reason for this is at the far eastern end of the station there used to be a footbridge which led to a pathway on the north side of the tracks. If you look north from the train as you travel eastbound, you might still see the path where people used to walk to enter and exit this end of the station.

South Ealing

Northfields and South Ealing are ridiculously close together and the train will travel between the two of them in under a minute – time it to see how many seconds it takes!

Uxbridge to Rayners Lane (see Metropolitan Line)

South Harrow

Serving an area historically known as Roxeth, the name South Harrow represents a wish to associate the station with a better known place name, a tendency of railway companies. The first thing to see here is the original but now disused station building which is at the southern end of the south-bound platform. This was used until 1935 when the new entrance on the main road was completed. The old building is still used by train staff, who sometimes go into here to use the toilet before continuing to drive the train.

Sudbury Hill

Sudbury Hill is a classic Holden style station with its bricks, glass and concrete. The staircases down to the platforms are very typical of brutalist 1930s architecture. Like many other of the less well known Holden stations, it has not aged well.

Sudbury Town

Whilst Sudbury Town is constructed from the same materials as Sudbury Hill, it is on another level and is my all-time favourite Underground station with its high ceiling and grand ticket hall. It's the only station to have a barometer inside (high up on the inside brick wall) and the original wooden passimeter (free-standing ticket office) is a joy to see, as is the seating area with wooden benches – totally unlike anything you'll see at a modern Underground station. Best of all, Sudbury Town has a unique font used all over the station – in the roundels, to the 'Way Out' and toilets signs. It's a serif-variant of the classic Johnston font normally used. Look closely to see the difference.

Alperton

Until recent years, Alperton station was one of only two stations that had an escalator going *up* to platform level; however you cannot see it anymore as it is now disused. It is blocked up behind a red door at both the bottom and the top – it took you to the eastbound platform.

Park Royal

Park Royal is not a Charles Holden designed station, even though many people think it is because it looks like one. Architects Herbert Welch and Felix Lander deliberately copied Holden's style – in particular the distinctive tower adjacent to the ticket hall. Like so many Underground stations it looks great lit up at night. Over on the westbound platform, see if you can find the 'Staff Letters' letterbox that is located here, from a time when train guards would carry internal mail around on trains.

North Ealing

As you enter this station just after the ticket barriers you either turn left for eastbound trains, or immediately walk down some steps for westbound trains – there is what looks like an old District Railway sign here saying 'To the trains' with a finger pointing the way. This however is not the original sign but a copy, and the 'real' one has been relocated in the main stairwell at the Underground's head office, 55 Broadway, SW1. The station has a lot of character nevertheless and is well worth a visit.

Ealing Common

Head out to the ticket office here and prepare to look in two directions. There is a brown plaque on the wall, from which you may want to look up at the beautiful stained-glass windows. Then, look down to spot the star shape on the floor of the ticket hall.

Acton Town (See District Line)

Hammersmith

Hammersmith station on first look is just part of a rebuilt shopping centre, and you may think there's nothing special about it at first, however there's a delightful thing to see here – and it's to do with time. Find any of the clocks that are at Hammersmith station (there are seven of them in total dotted all around the place), and study them closely. You'll see that the design has been based upon a Underground map, with green and blue lines used (the colour of the two lines that pass through here – the District and Piccadilly), and that 'station ticks' have been used to denote where the numbers are on the face of the clock, a lovely little piece of design.

Barons Court

A splendid 1905 building greets passengers arriving at this station. It was built that year when the District Railway opened the station. It anticipated the arrival of the Piccadilly Tube the following year. Note that there's no apostrophe here, unlike neighbouring Earl's Court. Barons Court, like Hammersmith and Acton Town, has cross-platform inter-change with the District Line (unlike at Earl's Court) so for people travelling to/from Heathrow Airport with heavy bags, this is a station to alight at if you're using the District Line to interchange with the Piccadilly Line. The gents' toilet near the ticket barriers gives a good view of the platforms. Notable too are the lovely green tiles in the ticket hall, the wooden benches on the platforms, and the 1930s train indicator on the eastbound Piccadilly Line platform.

Earl's Court

It was at this station that the first escalator on the Underground was installed, back in 1911. There's a staircase at the front end of the eastbound District Line platforms, a spiral staircase which is almost never used by any other passengers. This takes you straight down to the Piccadilly Line platforms, perfect for if you don't want to be squashed in with the crowds at rush hour!

Gloucester Road

At platform level here, the original style of tilework has been replicated incorporating 'Way Out' and 'No Exit' signs, a nice juxtaposition of corporate styles of the time. These will also be found on other Piccadilly platforms further along the line and on a few Bakerloo and Northern Line platforms. Coming from the west, Gloucester Road also has the first Leslie Green surface level building, nicely preserved.

Knightsbridge

You may have only ever entered or exited this station via the 'regular' entrance, and not the one that was specifically built to be right next to Harrods. So, if you've never done it, now is the time ... exit at the eastern end and you'll walk along a short corridor to reach their store. The design of metallic finish to the walls of the platforms is unique. The name of the station is unique in having six consecutive consonants in it.

Hyde Park Corner

As you leave Hyde Park Corner on the train heading east, put your face up close to the window and keep an eye out on the right-hand side for the abandoned and disused Down Street station. Its platforms have now been bricked up, so you can quite clearly see where the tunnel changes from the regular tube wall to a bricked-up wall – that's where the abandoned station is. There's even an emergency exit here, where passengers could be led through a gate and out onto the street via the old station. During the second world war, Down Street station was used by a war cabinet led by Winston Churchill, who sometimes slept there. It is the disused station that more people request to visit than any other. The street level building remains, with a pair of black doors leading to offices on the first floor and a metal door by which access for staff and booked groups is obtained to the subterranean parts.

Waterloo and King's Cross St Pancras are the two busiest Underground stations, with around 100 million passengers entering or exiting each per year.

Green Park

Making an interchange between the Piccadilly Line and the Jubilee Line? You'll walk down a long corridor – coloured with tiles – that you've probably walked down before numerous times. But take a close look at the tiles you'll note that at the Piccadilly end they are colour blue, and as you walk along, the distribution of the colour changes and more silver ones – until they're all silver ones.

Piccadilly Circus

Piccadilly Circus has a remnant of an old emergency spiral staircase that can be used as an interchange between the Piccadilly Lines and northbound Bakerloo Line platform (and in reverse). Follow the normal Way Out signs for the Piccadilly Line but before you get to the escalators there is a small sign saying 'Bakerloo Line' which if you follow takes you straight to the Bakerloo platforms – much quicker than if you follow the normal signs to the Bakerloo Line. In the large circular area under the road that is the station concourse there are two things to see – the first is the 'World Clock' showing times in different zones around the globe, and opposite that is a display that is a tribute to Frank Pick, who commissioned Charles Holden – the designer of this and many other Piccadilly Line stations. There is a roundel here lit up with Pick's name on it.

Leicester Square

The distance between Leicester Square and the next station, Covent Garden, is the shortest on the Underground, at 260 metres. From street level it would in almost all cases be quicker to walk between them. This also makes it the worst-value-for-money journey on the Underground if you pay a cash single for a Zone 1 to Zone 1 station.

Covent Garden

One of two stations along the line to feature an old 'Bullseye' style roundel – a complete red circular 'filled in' disc. You'll find it at the front end of the westbound platform, and it looks splendid. The station has twice in its history been proposed for closure, first in 1929 and then in the 1980s, but today is much busier.

Holborn

Holborn has four platforms, two for the Central Line and two for the Piccadilly Line, but there are in fact two more abandoned platforms here – Numbers 5 and 6 which used to be for the shuttle down to Aldwych which closed in 1994. There are two set of 'double white' doors at the top of the stairs to the eastbound platform. More interesting though is that if you go to the front end of the eastbound platform there is a set of double brown doors on the left. If you push your eye up against the crack between the doors you can peer into the old abandoned corridor with original tiling that leads to the old platforms.

Russell Square

This is a delightful Leslie Green designed station just off Russell Square itself and another station without any escalators. Most Leslie Green stations were built with just a ground and first floor, with the intention of selling the space above and letting other businesses build on top of the station, but this never happened here at Russell Square. Cross the road and look back to admire the station front in all its unspoilt glory.

King's Cross St Pancras

At King's Cross it is often best to ignore the official signs telling you which way to go to change lines! They often take you the long way round on purpose to spread out passenger congestion, so see if you can find the staircase at the end of the Piccadilly Line platforms (and top of the Northern Line escalators) that takes you up to the Victoria Line. There is also another lesser-used passageway that links the Piccadilly Line and the end of the northbound Northern Line platform. And then, just when you think you're done, follow the signs for the 'Pentonville Road' exit from the Victoria Line which takes you down a mustard-yellow coloured and lesser-used corridor. Here is a set of double doors where you can peer out onto the abandoned platforms of the old King's Cross Thameslink station, then go up the steps to admire a magnificent mosaic which combines both the London Transport roundel and British Rail 'double arrow' symbol all in one.

Caledonian Road and *Holloway Road*

The ticket office at Holloway Road is splendid, with ornate green tiling and old style 'Ticket office' signage, which is rarely seen on the network now. The platforms at both stations remain largely in the original Leslie Green style. One at Caledonian Road has a name sign in the original 1908 style.

Arsenal

The only station to be named after a football club, this used to be the stop to travel to for football games with Arsenal – until the stadium moved, and although many passengers still choose to come here it's not as busy as it used to be. Holloway Road and Highbury & Islington stations are now busier for fans travelling to the Emirates Stadium. However, a remnant of crowd control remains that was only ever used on match days – a divider along the corridor which allowed people to enter the station even when large numbers of people were leaving it, and vice versa.

Finsbury Park

At each end (and on both) of the Piccadilly platforms, there are tiled balloon mosaics on the track side of the Tube tunnel. These were added in the 1980s and originally ran all along the walls, probably because someone at the time believed that the first balloon flight in Britain took place here. In fact, the first one took place from Finsbury Square, in the City of London, not Finsbury Park.

Manor House, Turnpike Lane, Wood Green and Bounds Green

This next section of the Tube – north from Finsbury Park all the way to Cockfosters – was built as an extension to the line in the 1930s, with stations by architect Charles Holden. Each of the four stations along this section is uniquely outstanding and worth a visit, though the street level building at Manor House is one of the plainest on the system. Each has their own tiling colour scheme. The stations at Turnpike Lane, Wood Green and Bounds Green also have larger platform tunnels than those elsewhere, these being 23ft in diameter instead of the normal 21ft. Note the decorative ventilation grilles high up on the platform walls; each station has a different design relating to its name, designed by artist Harold Stabler.

Arnos Grove

Arnos Grove is a Grade II* listed station and is now a tribute to Charles Holden. Jump off the train, come through the gateline and you'll find yourself in a brilliant circular ticket hall. In the middle of this is a 'passimeter' – an old ticket booth – which has now been turned into an exhibition (almost a mini museum display) all about the architect.

Southgate

Southgate is another Charles Holden masterpiece – the escalator shaft, the circular ticket hall and the street level building being outstanding. The concrete roof and the 'antenna' in the middle are supported by a central column so that the outer part of the roof can lie on all-round windows. Southgate is the most northerly station in tunnel on the Underground and unusually the tube tunnel mouth can be seen from a platform. Don't ignore the shopping parade by the curving bus station as this was an integral part of Holden's design vision. Following England reaching the semi-final of the 2018 Football World Cup, Southgate station was renamed Gareth Southgate (after the team manager) for two days in July. The temporary re-signing was sponsored by the credit card company Visa.

Oakwood

Continuing with the distinct colour schemes of all the stations at the northern end of the Piccadilly Line, here the colour is turquoise, and it has been used in places you might not realise – exit outside the station and find the circular bench and you'll see that the same colour has been used here too, an excellent attention to detail easily missed. Oakwood was not the station's original name – it opened as Enfield West. Being halfway between Enfield and Barnet, East Barnet was also considered before opening. It was in 1938 that it got its own place name following a campaign by local residents.

Cockfosters

Stand in the middle of the ticket hall to admire its architecture. Explore all the different exits out of the station to see where they lead; then come back and on the platform area go and find the garden gnomes. Yes... gnomes, here in the flower beds on the platforms. Cockfosters is also very similar in design to Uxbridge station – so a Piccadilly Line train running the full length of the line is nicely 'bookended' by two similar-looking stations.

VICTORIA LINE

Opened in stages between 1968 and 1971, the Victoria Line was seen as a solution to relieve pressure on other Underground lines in London and open up new tube connections to north London. It was built with connectivity with other lines in mind and all but one of its sixteen stations (Pimlico) links up with another part of the rail network. Every station has a unique platform tiling 'motif' design; a lovely touch.

Brixton

Before you enter the station cross the road and turn to look at the LU roundel that adorns the front of the station – it's the largest that you'll see anywhere on the

Underground. There is a larger roundel at Dalston Junction, but that's for the Overground.

Stockwell

Here at Stockwell it is not immediately obvious what the tile motif design represents; then you may notice the tiny bit of orange – which is the beak of a swan. Across the street from Stockwell Underground station is the local pub 'The Swan', once a well-known local venue for live music in London but now more of a nightclub.

Vauxhall

The tiles at Vauxhall that are of most interest aren't the ones at platform level (which are a reference to the Vauxhall Gardens that once existed nearby). Instead, head to the exit up to the bus station and on the exterior wall of one set of steps there is a wall of black tiles – with every so often some small tiles with part of the Underground map.

Pimlico

If you exit by following the signs to the Rampayne Street entrance, at the top of the steps in the concrete floor is another Underground roundel, etched into the concrete. If you look up though above your head, you'll see a lit-up version that is in essence 'burning' into the concrete below. Also, the station name roundels at platform level are back-lit – a feature now unique on the Underground.

Victoria

The Underground gets very busy in the morning with many arrivals at the main line station in a short period of time and TfL recently upgraded and expanded its station to make it bigger and more accessible. A nice thing to see here is just away from the entrance between the Underground and the main line station – there are two old preserved tiled railway maps on the wall, one showing the long-distance and one showing the local suburban service of the London, Brighton and South Coast Railway.

Green Park

This was just a Piccadilly Line station right up until 1969 when the Victoria Line was completed to Victoria and then 1979 when the Jubilee Line started to come through here. If you walk a minute down Piccadilly eastward to Dover Street you can find a brown coloured grille next to a shop front, and on it a sign that is in tell-tale London Underground Johnston font! This is where the original entrance used to be.

Oxford Circus

We're back to tiles, and coloured tiles again. There's a subtle but clever design feature here – crossings of brown, red and light blue tiles in the ticket hall and on the platforms, showing that Oxford Circus is the place where the Bakerloo, Central and Victoria Lines all intersect.

Warren Street

If you have time, follow the maze pattern on the Victoria Line platforms here – it is a genuine maze and a journey to the centre and back is possible. So, referring back to the labyrinth designs mentioned earlier, this can be said to be the only station with two different mazes.

Euston

See if you can find the lesser-used spiral staircase here, which is halfway along the passageway that links the two Victoria Line platforms together at one end. Interestingly, there are 64 steps in total on it – even though the sign says there are 51, which is only the number of steps on the *spiral* part. Once you know about this lesser-used exit, you may find yourself using it instead of the busy escalators.

King's Cross St Pancras

Easily the most complicated Underground station on the network, when new entrances and ticket halls were completed in 2009 it opened up even more corridors. There is a quicker way to get between the Victoria Line and the Piccadilly and Northern Lines than the one advertised. Instead of following the signs, head for the main exit escalators, but before you get to them, turn right into a small passageway, which twists and takes you down some steps which to your left brings you out by the escalators to take you down to the Northern Line, or to your immediate right the entrance to the Piccadilly Line platforms. Also, it is worth stopping to look up in the ticket hall – here is a clock beneath which is a plaque, paying tribute to those who died in the terrible fire tragedy here in the 1980s. It reads "In memory of the thirty one people who lost their lives in the King's Cross Underground fire of 18th November 1987". One of the measures taken following the inquiry into that disaster was the elimination on the Underground of escalators with wooden treads.

Highbury & Islington

We've already mentioned disused Underground stations in the book and across the road from the current entrance is the 1904 building to the Great Northern & City Railway Highbury & Islington station, and looking splendid. Walk around the corner into Highbury Fields park and you can see the disused rear entrance of it too.

Finsbury Park

This station was not built by the Underground but by the main line railway above. The southbound platform is in a larger tunnel than is normal on tube platforms, as is the adjacent Piccadilly Line one. Both were made available when the service from Moorgate to Finsbury Park was diverted to the elevated platforms here in connection with the transfer of this stretch of line from the Underground to British Rail, the tube line having been built in the early 20th Century to main line dimensions.

Seven Sisters

Most Victoria Line trains here use platforms 3 and 5, but platform 4 is there too – used for terminating trains here that are going to the nearby depot at Northumberland Park. You might sometimes see a member of staff getting *on* a terminating train to be taken to the depot where they work.

Tottenham Hale

The lift here is very unusual as the doors for the way in are at 90-degrees to the doors you use to exit the lift – the only one I know of on the Underground.

Blackhorse Road

If you've never been outside Blackhorse Road station before, now is the time to do so. If you've passed through the station you will have seen the platform tiles of the black horse, but there is a much larger one outside.

Walthamstow Central

The original plan for the Victoria Line was to terminate it at Wood Street, one station beyond Walthamstow Central. Had that happened, Wood Street would have been the only station on the line in the open.

WATERLOO & CITY LINE

Opened in 1898, the Underground line that is just two stops long didn't become part of the Underground until 1994 – prior to that it was owned by British Rail. Even though I've covered its two stops (Bank and Waterloo) in the other lines, I have a special fondness for the W&C because it's so special.

The Greathead Shield remnants at Bank Station

At the Bank end of the Waterloo & City Line, follow the signs and walk along the corridor that takes you to the DLR (and not up to the exit/ticket hall/Central Line). Halfway along this corridor are the remnants of the tunnelling shield that was used to dig out the Waterloo & City Line. It was left here buried underground for many years, and only discovered in the 1980s when the passageway from the DLR was being dug. There is a small plaque here which notes this – thousands of people walk past every day and probably don't ever notice it.

Part of it is in the open ... almost

The W&C service is entirely underground, so how do they get trains in and out when they need to? The answer lies around the corner from Waterloo station on Spur Road, where there is a gate with a path down to an opening covered up with a grille. Peer down into here and below you'll see the tracks and possibly a carriage or two. There is a blue coloured crane here – used for lifting in and out maintenance equipment – but when one of the carriages needs to be removed, it

involves closing off the nearby roads, and a specialised crane on a truck being brought in.

It is worked as part of the Central Line

The rolling stock currently used on the line is 1992 Tube Stock, as used on the Central Line, but instead of being 8-cars long, just 4-car trains are used. The W&C is also operated by drivers based from Leytonstone – a Central Line depot. We like to think that if the Underground map ever runs out of colours, they could use the turquoise colour of the W&C elsewhere, and just colour the Waterloo & City in red as a branch of the Central Line.

It almost had a third station

The line has always been a possible candidate for extension, or possibly having a third station placed along because it runs directly beneath Blackfriars station. If you ever find yourself at Blackfriars waiting for the District Line, bear in the mind that the Waterloo & City is just a few metres below your feet. It will most likely never happen as at peak hours the line is already running to capacity and it is doing what it was built to do – connect the City area of London with main line trains into Waterloo.

Filming Location

As the line is closed on Sundays, it makes the perfect place for use as a set for TV and Films, such as the 1998 film 'Sliding Doors' where it was dressed as Embankment station.

The only inclined walkway on the tube

The connection to the Waterloo & City Line from the main concourse has one of only two moving walkways on the tube and the only one that is inclined. The other walkway, not sloped, is at Waterloo.

Bibliography

Badsey-Ellis, A., *Underground Heritage* (Capital Transport 2012)

Badsey-Ellis, A., *The Hampstead Tube* (Capital Transport 2007)

Barker, T.C., and Robbins, M., *A History of London Transport Vols 1 & 2* (Allen & Unwin 1963/1974)

Bownes, D., Green, O., and Mullins, S., *Underground: How the Tube shaped London* (Allen Lane 2012)

Brown, J., *London Railway Atlas* (Ian Allan 2006)

Chernaik, J. (Ed.), *Poems on the Underground: A New Edition* (Penguin 2012)

Connor, J. E., *London's Disused Underground Stations* (Capital Transport 2012)

Croome, D.F., and Jackson, A.A., *Rails Through the Clay* (Capital Transport 1993)

Day, J. R., and Reed, J., *The Story of London's Underground* (Capital Transport 2010)

Emmerson, A., and Beard, T., *London's Secret Tubes* (Capital Transport 2004)

Emmerson A., *Tube Trivia* (Capital History, 2013)

Garland, K., *Mr Beck's Underground Map* (Capital Transport 1994)

Glover, J., *Principles of London Underground Operations* (Ian Allan 2000)

Gregg, J., *The Shelter of the Tubes* (Capital Transport 2001)

Halliday, S., *Underground to Everywhere* (Sutton Publishing 2001)

Harris, C.M., *What's in a Name?* (Capital History 2005)

Horne, M.A.C., *The Piccadilly Tube* (Capital Transport 2007)

Jackson, A.A., *London's Metropolitan Railway* (David & Charles 1986)

Jackson, A.A., *London's Metroland* (Capital History 2006)

Lawrence, D., *Bright Underground Spaces* (Capital Transport 2008)

Leboff, D., *London Underground Stations* (Ian Allan 1994)

Long, D., *The Little Book of the London Underground* (History Press 2009)

Ovenden, M., *London Underground by Design* (Penguin 2012)

Pedroche, Ben, *Do Not Alight Here* (Capital History, 2013)

Wolmar, C., *The Subterranean Railway* (Atlantic 2004)